Dubitskaya Natalia

Ceramic production in Belarus (VII century B.C. - 1 millennium A.D.)

Dubitskaya Natalia

Ceramic production in Belarus (VII century B.C. - 1 millennium A.D.)

ScienciaScripts

Imprint

Any brand names and product names mentioned in this book are subject to trademark, brand or patent protection and are trademarks or registered trademarks of their respective holders. The use of brand names, product names, common names, trade names, product descriptions etc. even without a particular marking in this work is in no way to be construed to mean that such names may be regarded as unrestricted in respect of trademark and brand protection legislation and could thus be used by anyone.

Cover image: www.ingimage.com

This book is a translation from the original published under ISBN 978-620-2-06708-9.

Publisher:
Sciencia Scripts
is a trademark of
Dodo Books Indian Ocean Ltd. and OmniScriptum S.R.L publishing group

120 High Road, East Finchley, London, N2 9ED, United Kingdom
Str. Armeneasca 28/1, office 1, Chisinau MD-2012, Republic of Moldova, Europe
Printed at: see last page
ISBN: 978-620-7-92189-8

Table of Contents

H. N. Dubitskaya

Ceramic production in the lands of Belarus in the 7th century BC. - I millennium.

T.I. Levkova is dedicated

Introduction

The paper deals with the issues of ceramic ware manufacturing technology in the territory of Belarus in the Iron Age and early Middle Ages. Ceramics is the most massive archaeological material in the cultural layer of ancient monuments. It carries considerable information of cultural, chronological and to some extent ethnic character and is one of the most reliable material sources, especially when studying the pre-written period. In addition, ceramics is the first man-made material, and ceramic production is one of the oldest specialized industries. Special attention is paid to technical and technological schemes related to the selection of raw materials, composition of molding masses, and firing conditions. For the first time in Belarusian archeology, extensive research on ancient pottery with the use of natural science methods allowed to restore the history of ancient pottery in Belarus with much greater accuracy. The research was carried out according to the methodology developed specially for archaeological ceramics by T. I. Levkova.

Belarusian archaeologists showed interest in the technological peculiarities of ancient pottery production even in the pre-war years. The descriptions of ceramic material by A. N. Lyavdanski, A. D. Kovaleni, S. A. Dubinski, and V. Golubovich were particularly thorough. They tried to emphasize the technological peculiarities of the composition of ceramic masses, as well as the conditions and peculiarities of the firing of products, as much as visual observation and the level of development of special knowledge about ceramics allowed. The interest in the technical and technological aspect of the study of ceramic production increased especially in the post-war years. Nevertheless, despite the fact that ancient ceramics, including ceramics of the Iron Age, was the object of study of a number of archaeologists (Y. V. Kukharenko, P. N. Tretyakov, O. N. Melnikovskaya, L. D. Pobolya), it was not possible to trace the history of the development of ceramic production. The main reason was the lack of a deep and complete study of the technological features of ceramics using a variety of modern research methods. Except in some cases (A. A. Bobrinsky, O. Y. Krug, M. I. Loshenkov, M. A. Kulkova), the technological aspects of pottery production were still considered on the basis of visual observations, which greatly reduced the reliability of the results and made it impossible to trace the history of the development of ceramic production.

The paper focuses on materials from archaeological sites of the Belarusian Podneprovye and Polesie. Conducting such studies of materials from the territory of Belarus allows us to compare them with simultaneous materials from other regions, the study of which was carried out in other laboratories. Thus, these materials can be included in the broad scheme of studies of ceramic production in Eastern Europe.

This paper reflects the process of formation, further development, cultural and production continuity of pottery of the Early Iron Age and Early Middle Ages cultures in Belarus. The production of pottery in Belarus began already in the Neolithic Age (IV-III millennia BC). Pottery was molded manually, without the use of a potter's wheel. However, already at the earliest stage the production of ceramic tableware was a rather developed specialized production. In the Neolithic and Bronze Age potters were well oriented in the quality of ceramic clays, preferring, based on the existing technical possibilities and availability of natural raw materials, easily fusible clays of lake-alluvial genesis (Upper Podneprovie, Polesie). In Podvinje, in the north of Belarus, strongly sandy lake-glacial clay rocks prevailed. For the compositions of molding masses, such artificial thickening components as crystalline rock sands and crushed pottery (fireclay) were widely used. The schemes based on sod and fireclay are the oldest local technological schemes.

Iron Age pottery is characterized by significant continuity with previous production schemes. The knowledge and skills on the technology of molding masses preparation and firing obtained at one stage were preserved and were one of the components of the pottery traditions of the next stage. The change of technological traditions was gradual. At the same time, it is a significant leap in its development, based on new techno-

technological possibilities, allowing to raise pottery to a higher stage of specialized work. It was during the Early Iron Age that, as a result of further differentiation and specialization of ceramic production, special forms of labor organization emerged, which can be characterized as pre-craft.

§ 1 Production of pottery among the tribes of the Milograd culture (7th-3rd centuries B.C.).

The Milograd culture is one of the oldest archaeological cultures of the Early Iron Age in Belarus. The time of its existence is VII-III centuries BC. The monuments of the Milograd culture were introduced into the scientific turnover in the 50s thanks to the researches of O.N. Melnikovskaya [Melnikovskaya, 1967]. Milograd antiquities were also studied by L.D. Pobol, M.I. Lolnikovskaya [Melnikovskaya, 1967]. Pobol, M.I. Loshenkov, A.A. Egoreychenko, S.E. Rassadin [Egoreychenko, 1996; Loshenkov, 1990; 1999; 2011; Pobol, 1983; Rassadin, 1989]. The area of distribution of monuments of the Milograd culture in the territory of modern Belarus occupies the eastern part of the Pripyat Polesie and the south of the Dnieper basin, including the lower reaches of the Berezina River.

The production of ceramic tableware by the tribes of the Milograd culture was already a sufficiently developed production with established technological schemes. Milograd craftsmen possessed a certain amount of necessary knowledge about clay, about the possibility and necessity of its heating for obtaining special molding masses that best met the required technological parameters. In spite of the fact that firing was carried out without special heat engineering equipment, its controllability becomes higher (obtaining a stable gas environment, observing the necessary temperature regime). All this indicates a rather high professional level of Milograd potters.

Milograd potters, as well as in the previous epoch, continued to use easily fusible medium plastic (the share of natural non-plastic admixture usually 15-25 %), mainly hydrous-mica clays by their mineral composition. In some cases and only for making miniature vessels lean lake-glacial clayey rocks (loams) were used. The widespread use of hydrosludic lake-alluvial clays of the Anthropogenic period has a solid technical basis. Firstly, such clays are widespread, and it is not difficult to find their outcrops near settlements. Secondly, taking into account the ancient methods of firing, i.e. fire firing with its low firing temperatures (up to 850°C), easily melting clays were necessary. This is the reason why high quality kaolinite clay rocks requiring higher temperatures - over 900°C - were not used. Apparently, refractory kaolinite clay was used only for the production of technical ceramics (crucibles, benches).

It was during this period that a common technological scheme for different regions of the Milograd tribes (Upper Podneprovie, Polesie) was formed - the recipe for molding mass: clay + tarmac + fireclay. Recipes with a new type of special ottoshchitel (crushed bog iron ore) appear. Simple recipes (clay + tarmac, clay + fireclay) began to disappear, and they were replaced by complex multi-component recipes based on clay and several types of special opacifier. There is a standardization of methods of molding mass heating - the ratio of non-plastic (natural and artificial heating agent) and plastic (clay binder) parts in the composition of the molding mass is approximately 1 : 2.5. Firing technology is characterized by the stability of relatively low temperatures (500-750°C) and reducing gas environment.

The compositions of molding masses of Milograd vessels are characterized by the presence of special calcifying impurities of inorganic origin. The oldest artificial impurity, widely spread in pottery in Belarus, is the crystalline rock tresva. As an initial raw material for obtaining, as a rule, used ordinary biotite granite - a rock quite widespread in pebble and boulder material in the territory of Belarus and the most easily amenable to crushing because of its physical and mechanical properties. Granite tarmac includes fragments of the initial rock, and also grains of mineral components of granite, isolated at crushing. It is mainly feldspars, quartz, biotite, less often muscovite. The grains were crushed as finely as possible, usually the size of grains did not exceed 2-3 mm, the maximum size of grains is up to 5-7 mm. The share of the sands in the molding mass fluctuated depending on the plasticity of the initial clay rock and the presence of other special peeling components from 5 to 15 %. Chippings were not only the oldest, but also the leading special peeling additive in pottery in Belarus. Sharp-angular inclusions of the loam created a kind of rigid frame of the vessel, which is especially important for hand molding, loam helped to keep the shape of the vessel during drying. These qualities allowed dried cobbler to gain a stable foothold in ancient pottery for a long time.

The second type of special peeling additive, widely represented in Milograd pottery, was chamot. Chamotte, like tarmac, has local roots in pottery in Belarus and was known as far back as the Bronze Age potters. Its appearance is recorded both at the monuments of the Pripyat Polesie (Ozernoye) and Upper Podneprovye (Prorva). The main source for this additive, judging by the degree of amorphization of clay matter in their composition, was crushed ceramic slaughter or waste from ceramic production. In contrast to other special ottomashing inorganic admixtures, chamotte by its nature is related to the clay mass, which allows it to interact with it better. The peculiarity of this additive is that chamotte can be ground very finely. The fine particles of fireclay "blur" into the surrounding mass, which also implies that they interact even more with the main substrate during the firing of the product. It is also important that these properties of fireclay allowed to soften the "stiffness" of pebbles, which undoubtedly contributed to obtaining a better quality shard. As it was said, fireclay was ground rather finely, the maximum size of fireclay inclusions did not exceed 2-3 mm. The share of fireclay particles in complex recipes in the molding mass of Milograd vessels averaged 3-5%. This is in the case if fireclay occupied the second position after tarmac. In simple recipes (clay + fireclay) and in complex ones, when fireclay prevailed over tarmac, the share of fireclay reached 10-15 %.

In Mylohrad pottery at about the middle and late stages of the culture's existence (IV-III centuries B.C.) a new type of special inorganic peeling agent appears - crushed bog iron ore. This type of oatmeal additive was recorded at this time both at the Mylohrad monuments of the Pripyat Polesie (Lemeshevichi) and in the Upper Pidniprovye (Rassvet, Lyubny, Horodok, Otruby). Ore was always a minor additive and is found only in complex recipes. Apparently, crushed bog ore performed the same functions as fireclay, i.e. it was a "soft" opacifier. The fine degree of crushing of the material, as in the case of fireclay, predetermined a rather strong interaction with the clay mass. Obviously, it is the similarity of technical qualities of these two types of special oatmealizing additives that explains the fact that they are rarely found in the same recipe. In any case, they are never recorded together in Milograd pottery. The share of crushed bog ore, as well as chamotte, in the composition of the molding mass also varied on average 3-5 %. The size of the largest ore inclusions did not exceed 0.5-0.6 mm.

For the Early Milograd complex of the Pripyat Polesie (Lemeshevichi) a special calcifying additive in the form of carefully calibrated coarse and coarse-grained (up to 1.3 mm) quartz sand in the amount of 15-18 % was recorded. Such a special admixture was not noted in the Milograd pottery of the Upper Sub-Dnieper region.

The most ancient technological schemes in Milograd pottery, the origins of which should be sought in the previous epoch, are the schemes based on clay binder and dresva and clay binder and chamotte. The oldest recipe, with its roots in Neolithic pottery, is the clay + tarmac recipe. The presence of driftwood in the molding mass is also noted at all other Neolithic sites in Belarus [Isayenko, 1972, p. 51; Kalechits, 1994, p. 1384 CharniauskC979, pp. 55, 61].

The scheme based on clay binder and chamotte appears in the Pripyat Polesie in the Early Bronze Age (Ozernoye, Oressa river). Apparently, the appearance of this recipe in the Upper Podneprovye region belongs to the same time or somewhat later. Most likely, the appearance of chamotte in pottery in Belarus is not an introduced tradition, in particular from the southern forest-steppe territories, where it was widespread. The use of chamotte as a special calcifying additive is a consequence of the development of the local technological tradition. It was caused by the need to soften the "stiffness" of the pebbles. Finely ground fireclay was ideal for this purpose. The widespread use of finely ground fireclay is noted already in Milograd pottery.

Recipes based on dresva and chamotte as special calcifying additives existed in parallel. However, recipes using fireclay alone were apparently never mass-produced. In mixed recipes, fireclay usually acted as a non-core calcifying additive. It should be noted that in Milograd pottery simple recipes based on clay binder and dresva or chamotte are fading. They are replaced already in the early Milograd time by a complex recipe formed on their basis: clay + loam + chamotte. Gradually this tradition acquired the features of a stable technological scheme and, occupying a dominant position in the pottery of the Milograd culture tribes, pushed aside simple unmixed recipes.

However, the tradition of using simple recipes continued to exist and undoubtedly coexisted with complex recipes for a long time, which demonstrates its stable conservatism.

As a rule, the leading special peeling additive in the composition of a complex recipe was usually sanddark, fireclay was in the second position. However, chamotte was not always a secondary additive. In a number of cases, the share of fireclay exceeds that of burr, and this is characteristic not only for the Pripyat Polesie, but also in the Upper Podniprovye, especially in its southern part (Staroye Krasnoye, Lyubny, Lipnyaki). This diversity is explained on the one hand by the proximity of the "fireclay" forest-steppe and the influence of pottery of the Scythian circle cultures, and on the other hand by the incomplete formation of the tradition itself.

The recipe of clay + clay+dresva + chamotte is common for the whole Milograd pottery. In the Upper Podneprovie it was formed on the basis of the merger of two simple recipes clay + tarmac and clay + fireclay at the early and middle stages of the Milograd culture (VII-IV centuries BC). In Pripyat Polesie the process of its formation goes back to an earlier period - pottery of the Bronze Age. In particular, its presence is recorded at the Bronze Age settlement Ozernoye.

The tradition of making molding masses with bog iron ore, apparently, has no "roots" in the pottery of the tribes of previous archaeological cultures. At the same time, it should hardly be regarded as introduced from outside. The recipe based on clay binder dresva and crushed bog iron ore appears in Milograd pottery in its middle and late stages (Rassvet, Lyubny, Gorodok, Otruby, Lemeshevichi) - IV-III centuries BC. Most likely, this is a local tradition, which emerged on the basis of the expansion of ideas about new peeling materials. In order to oatomize the molding mass, bog ore was thoroughly crushed or earthy ore was used. The finer size reduction favored a more uniform distribution in the mass and thus a better interaction with it. Usually, this leaning agent was introduced into the ceramic mass in small quantities, because in large quantities it has a negative effect on the properties of the mass. Crushed ore was always included in the mixed recipe as a secondary additive and apparently, like fireclay, served as a "soft" tenderizer.

In Pripyat Polesie in the Early Milograd complex of the Lemeshevichi settlement a recipe based on clay and carefully calibrated sand was recorded. The use of quartz sand for clay mass ottification is quite typical for the Scythian cultures of the forest-steppe zone. Most likely, the tradition of using sand for sanding the molding mass in pottery in Belarus has a southern origin. However, the small number of such recipes testifies to its insignificant influence on the local ceramic production.

Among the non-main single recipes in Milograd pottery is also a recipe for making molding mass from one natural clay without artificial additives (Liski). The starting material was lean clay, close to loams, with natural clastic part of which was not less than 35-40 %. Such clays were used only for molding miniature vessels.

Milograd potters fired dishes on fire pits. Firing in fire pits is the most typical and the most widespread method of firing on the territory of the forest belt of Eastern Europe in the Iron Age. Nevertheless, using the simplest firing devices, the potters of Milograd obtained sufficiently high quality ware meeting the necessary consumer characteristics.

Fire firing is evidenced by low temperatures, which, judging by the degree of clay substance alteration, varied in the range of 500-700 (750)°C. It was the campfire firing that caused the use of easy-melting clays of predominantly hydrous mica mineral composition. The use of such clays allowed the Milograd potters to produce sufficiently strong tiles at low temperatures (up to 800--850°C).

The gas environment, in which the firing of Milograd vessels took place, was defined as oxidizing - with a sufficient supply of air oxygen, and reducing - with an excess of carbon. The use of two firing modes testifies to a significant level of skill of Milograd potters, as it is extremely difficult to regulate the firing mode in the conditions of the fire. As a rule, preference was given to reduction firing. This is due to the fact that in a reducing gas environment the sintering process goes deeper than in an oxidizing environment at the same temperature. In a reducing environment, less fuel is needed, fuel quality requirements are not so strict, and most importantly, reducing firing is easier to control. The wide application of reduction firing in Milograd pottery was a stable technological tradition with ancient roots in the pottery of previous epochs. Such a stable existence is predetermined and directly derived from the fire firing.

Throughout the entire existence of the Milograd culture (7th-3rd centuries B.C.), complex changes took place in the technology of ceramic production. They are connected not only with the accumulation of production material, but also with the beginning of the formation of new principles and conditions for the organization of specialized labor. New forms of craft production gradually replaced the domestic production, which had developed and flourished during this period.

A technical and technological indicator in the pottery of the Milograd tribes, testifying to the origin of the craft, is the creation of a region-wide technological scheme based on clay binder, tars and chamotte, standardization of molding masses. It is she who played the main role in further deepening of labor specialization.

Two main stages can be distinguished in the development of ceramic production among the tribes of the Milograd culture. The first stage is connected mainly with the quantitative accumulation of technical and technological knowledge, the second stage - with the gradual transition of the accumulated quantity into a new quality.

The first stage is the formation and flourishing of domestic production (VII - early III centuries BC). During this period there is a further use of traditional and formation of new technological schemes. A common technological scheme for different regions of settlement of the Milograd tribes - the recipe of clay + tares + fireclay - is formed. The standardization of methods of molding masses washing takes place. In firing technology the search for optimal modes is carried out.

The second stage is the emergence of elements of craft production (III century B.C.). During this period the improvement of technical methods continues. The creation of products with high consumer characteristics in conditions of primitive technical base can testify to the emergence of masters of high qualification - potters-professionals.

The creation of a common technological scheme for all regions of the Milograd culture unified the technological process in Milograd pottery. Identification of single recipes with the presence of other special oatmealizing admixtures, such as the recipe of clay + sand in Pripyat Polesie, in no way changes the general trend of functioning and development of Milograd pottery as a whole.

§ 2 Production of pottery among the tribes of the Zarubinets culture in Belarus (II century BC - I century AD).

The Zarubinets culture (2nd century B.C. - 1st century A.D.) is the closest to the West European cultures of the Middle Iron Age in terms of the overall relatively high level of production, abundance of metal in everyday life and other indicators. Ceramic tableware is characterized by a special peculiarity. All Zarubinets pottery is divided into two main categories according to the methods of surface treatment: lobed and unlobed ware. If the glossy ware, especially of careful workmanship, prevailed at burial sites, the settlements are characterized by unglossed ware. Fluted vessels from settlements are usually characterized by a slightly worse quality of surface treatment. Vessels whose surface is only slightly glazed, the so-called underglazed pottery, are not uncommon. Such a significant difference in the character of surface treatment of vessels in settlements and burial grounds is explained by their purpose. Roughly dressed and underglazed vessels served as everyday kitchen utensils, while glazed pottery was used as tableware and for ritual purposes.

The area of distribution of classical Zarubinets monuments on the territory of Belarus is the Pripyat Polesie (Pripyat variant) and the southern part of the Belarusian Podneprovie, up to the mouth of the Berezina River (Upper Dnieper variant). To the north of the Berezina River mouth, the descendants of the classical Zarubinets began to settle from the turn of the A.D. (post-Zarubinets monuments). Settling along the Dnieper and its tributaries, the Zarubinets came into direct contact with the preceding population of the Milograd culture. At the turn of the 3rd - 2nd centuries B.C., the Milograd culture was at the stage of its extinction. Nevertheless, the descendants of the Milograd culture played not the least role in the formation of the Belarusian variants of the Zarubinets culture, including the development of ceramic production technology. Zarubinets potters borrowed local technological schemes, which later replaced the schemes they had previously used. The main technological scheme in Zarubinets pottery, as in Milograd time, is the recipe of clay + tares + fireclay.

As an initial clay raw material, Zarubinets potters, as a rule, used the same medium-plastic lake-alluvial clays of anthropogenic origin, mainly of hydrosludic or hydrosludic-montmorillonite mineral composition. In some cases, especially in Pripyat Polesie, kaolinite component may be present. At the same time, the use of clays with kaolinite content in fire firing is undesirable, so such clays, despite their high technical characteristics, were usually rejected.

Sometimes Zarubinets potters still used highly plastic clay rocks. Such raw materials were recorded at the Chaplin settlement and burial site in the south of Belarus. To the south of Chaplin village, near which the archaeological monument is located, along the Dnieper bank there are known outcrops of Neogene and Upper Paleogene clays. Such clayey rocks containing a significant admixture of montmorillonite and mixed hydrosludic-montmorillonite materials were used by ancient potters for the production of lacquered and mostly unlacquered tableware. The share of natural clastic material in them did not exceed 3-10 %. Also only for unglazed ware in Chaplin were used clays from the second claying area - ordinary, mainly hydrous mica in its mineral composition of medium plastic clay rocks (the share of natural clastic admixture up to 35-40 %). Also one of miniature vessels was molded from lean lake-glacial clayey rocks, clastic natural admixture in which reached 60% (loam).

Judging by Chaplin's materials, highly plastic with high content of clayey rocks were used for the production of both chipped and unchipped tableware, medium plastic, mainly hydrous mica clayey rocks - only for unchipped tableware. Although, for example, at the settlement of David-Horod (Pripyat Polesie), where the use of clays from two clay pits with different degrees of natural clastic admixture in their composition was also recorded, such a preference was not observed. There, clays from both claystones were used to the same extent for the production of both unflaked and flaked ware. In general, for the manufacture of thin-walled and flaked tableware and ritual ware, more stringent requirements were imposed on the clay raw material: clays were thoroughly mixed, sorted from coarse inclusions, and special admixtures were introduced in finely ground form.

Zarubinets potters in the territory of Belarus used the same special thickening additives of inorganic origin as the Milograd potters to make molding masses. The main peeling additive was granite tarmac. Cobbles of crystalline rocks were obtained by crushing boulders and pebbles to different sizes, judging by the significant secondary changes of feldspars and biotite in the composition of the cobbles, weathered granite boulders easily amenable to crushing were selected for its production. Sometimes biotite gneiss, unstable sandstones were used for obtaining gravel. To refine the ceramic mass for lacquered vessels, carefully crushed loam was used, in which the maximum size of inclusions did not exceed 1.5-2.0 mm. The degree of pulverization of the unbroken vessels was not so thorough, sometimes inclusions reached up to 4,5-5,0 mm in cross-section. The share of the sands in the composition of the molding masses of Zarubinets vessels on average from 5 to 20 %. The lowest content of the gravel was recorded at the settlement David-Horodok (southern part of the right bank of the Pripyat Polesie) - 2-5 %, maximum 10%. This is due to the fact that the southern "fireclay" tradition dominates in the pottery of David-Horodok, and the sulphur usually occupies the second position. The highest content of 15-20% was recorded in the composition of molding masses of Chaplin Zarubinets vessels (south of the Belarusian Podneprovye region). The addition of such a large amount of special otoschitel testifies to the high plasticity of the initial clay rocks, which is typical for Chaplin, because the ratio of non-plastic and plastic parts in the composition of molding masses of Zarubinets vessels remained as in the Milograd time - 1:2.5.

Chamot or ceramic otoshchitel, as a special otoshchitelnye additive, was widespread in Zarubinets pottery. Moreover, the further south one went, the share of chamotte increased. Especially strong positions of chamotte in the 2nd century BC. - turn of the AD were in the Pripyat Polesie. This is most likely due to the powerful southern impulse, which was brought by the Zarubin people settling up the Dnieper and its tributaries. As before, pottery was used to produce fireclay, as evidenced by the results of double firing of fireclay particles. To obtain fireclay, dried clay was also used, pre-fired at temperatures lower than the firing temperature of the products. In Pripyat Polesie (David-Gorod) for obtaining ceramic otoshchitel we used products from relatively refractory clays (hydrous mica with admixture of kaolinite-motnmorillonite components), the structure of which is weakly disturbed by repeated firing. The share of chamotte in the compositions of molding masses of Zarubinets vessels, depending on the plasticity of the clay binder and the presence of other calcifying additives usually did not exceed 3-5 %. The exception is David-Gorodok, in the pottery of which fireclay was the leading additive - up to 10%. The particle size of fireclay did not exceed 2.5-3.0 mm, most often up to 1.0-1.5 mm. The finely ground ceramic opacifier "blurs" in the molding mass, thus improving its technological qualities.

In the Zarubinets pottery on a number of monuments, crushed bog iron ore continues to be used as an additional special leaning admixture. The tradition of using crushed ore may have been borrowed by the Zarubinets potters from the local population of the Milograd culture. Although it is possible that the Zarubinets brought it with them. In any case, such admixture is known in the Zarubinets pottery of the Middle Sub-Dnieper region. However, S. P. Pachkova, who studied the Zarubinets ceramics of the Middle Sub-Dnieper region, believes that this additive was not special, but natural. She argues that the content of ore in the total volume of the mass is insignificant, its addition to the molding mass is not typical for Zarubinets pottery [Pachkova, 1974, p. 114]. One can disagree with this point of view: ore was always a secondary special additive and was introduced in small quantities. By its technical characteristics finely ground ore is similar to finely ground chamotte, i.e. it is a "soft" opacifier softening the hard properties of tarmac. In the Middle Piedmont the addition of ore in the molding mass of Zarubinets vessels was detected at four monuments (Pilipenkova Gora, Pirogov, Velikie Dmitrovichi, Lyutezh), both in uncoated and coated ware. Among the studied samples, ore was found in 36 cases out of 200 (18 %), among the broken ware - in 12 cases out of 150 (8.5 %) [Pachkova, 1974, p. 114], so it is hardly possible to speak about the random nature of this impurity.

In the Upper Sub-Dnieper region especially widely used ore for ot ot otification of molding masses by the potters of Chaplin settlement both for the production of lacquered and unlacquered ware. The share of bog ore in the composition of molding masses of Chaplin vessels was 3-10 %, sometimes 15 %. In general for Zarubinets vessels the amount of specially introduced additive, such as crushed marsh ore, varied in the composition of molding masses, as well as in Milograd vessels within 3-5 %. Such a significant amount of ore in the molding mass of Chaplin vessels, obviously, depended on the quality of the initial highly plastic clayey rocks, which were characterized by a low content of natural clastic admixture - up to 3-10 %. For thinner hydrosludic clays such amount of ore in the composition of molding masses is inexpedient. Ore for the purpose of adding to the ceramic mass, as in the Milograd time, was ground quite finely, up to powdery state, although there are, especially in kitchen vessels, quite large inclusions - up to 1.5-2.0 mm, in isolated cases up to 4.0 mm.

In the Zarubinets time in the Pripyat pottery appears such a type of otoshchitel as dried clay or fragments of unburnt vessels (Velemichi II, Lemeshevichi, Otverzhichi, Remel, Lemeshevichi, Horodishche). The clay otoshchitel was inclusions of dried clay coils. These are rolls of tin or non-tin clay of dense packing, practically without admixture of silty clay. Sometimes refractory kaolinite-montmorillonite clays were used for this purpose, the structure of which changes slightly during fire firing. The particle size of clay otoshchitel is up to 1.0-1.2 mm. Their share in the composition of molding masses is about 3%.

The tradition of using clay otoshchitel is of southern origin. Its use is not typical for the Upper Dnieper pottery. During firing at low temperatures this type of opacifier provided almost simultaneous temperature transformations of the clay mass and opacifier, i.e. it was a soft plastic opacifier.

The tradition of using sand as a special peeling component is also of southern origin. In ancient pottery in Belarus, the use of sand as a special additive is reliably recorded only in the Pripyat Polesie. Recipes based on the addition of sand are very common in the ceramic production of the forest-steppe zone in the Bronze Age and Early Iron Age and connect the local Pripyat tradition with the production schemes of the southern neighbors. This type of special ottoman is not characteristic of the pottery of the Upper Podneprovie. Its use is recorded as a single case in the Early Milograd pottery at the

Polesian villages (Lemeshevichi).

A. A. Bobrinsky and O. Y. Krug point out the use of quartz sand as one of the most widespread special protectants in the compositions of ceramic masses of Zarubinets vessels of Pripyat Polesie. In particular, O. Y. Krug notes that during the manufacture of vessels at the Otverzhichi burial ground 10-15 % of quartz sand and 15-20 % of chamotte were added to the dough of lacquered vessels, and about 20 % of sand and 20 % of chamotte to the dough of unlacquered vessels [Kasparova, 1976, p. 35-66]. The addition of fine sand is recorded in the compositions of molding masses of lobed and unlobed vessels in Velimichi-2 [Kasparova, 1972, 53-111] and Remel [Kasparova, 1987, p. 52-70]. The sand was usually carefully sorted before being used as a special otoshchitel, which distinguishes it from unsorted natural sandy-silty admixture. Nevertheless, it is not always possible to completely separate natural sandy-siltstone from specially introduced impurities of mineral origin, in particular sand. Taking into account this fact, it should be recognized that sand as an artificial peeling additive in pottery of Pripyat Polesie in the Early Iron Age was used much less frequently than it was previously thought.

In the Middle Dnieper Zarubinets pottery, along with inorganic otoshchitel, organic otoshchitel was widely used. This is, first of all, crushed stems of plants, cereal grains, sometimes crushed bones [Pachkova, 1974, p. 113]. Organic otoshchitel was used quite often by Zarubinets potters of Polesie (Remel, Velemichi-2, Otverzhichi, Semuradtsy) [Kasparova, 1972, p. 69; 1976, pp. 48-49   ; 1987, p. 67; Pobol, 1969, p. 121]. However, it is difficult to   judge the technical significance of this type of otoshchitel because there are no quantitative data on its content in the molding mass. For the Zarubinets ceramics of the Belarusian Podneprovye region organic otoshchitel, apparently, is not characteristic. Only in one sample of ceramics from Chaplin an addition of crushed bones was recorded, the content of which did not exceed 1 %, which does not allow it to be considered as a special otoshchitel. The admixture of crushed plants, as a special opacifier capable of changing the properties of the molding mass, is also not characteristic of the Iron Age ceramics of the Upper Podneprovye region.

Pottery in the tribes of the Zarubinets culture is characterized, on the one hand, by the preservation and further development of traditional techniques, on the other hand, by the appearance of new techniques associated with the introduction of new technological traditions into local pottery. For the Zarubinets pottery in Belarus, as well as in the Milograd time, the recipes based on clay binder with the addition of crystalline rock grit and chamotte are characteristic. Along with simple recipes: clay + tarmac and clay + chamotte, the complex recipe: clay + tarmac + chamotte, the origins of which should be sought in the pottery of the Bronze Age (Kryvaltsesch, 1999, p. 42-43), became widespread. As a region-wide recipe it was formed in the Milograd time at the middle stage of cultural development. It was in the Zarubinets time that the process of substitution of traditions of composing simple recipes for molding masses and formation of complex recipes on their basis was completed. Regarding the complex all-regional recipe: clay + tarmac + fireclay, in contrast to the Milograd time in Zarubinets pottery in the composition of this recipe there is a change of priorities. If in Mylohrad pottery the main component was always granite woodcrete, the Zarubinets potters of Pripyat Polesie in some cases favored fireclay. This is due to the powerful southern "chamotte" impulse, which was brought by the Zarubinets. At the same time in Polesie there was also a significant influence of the Upper Dnieper traditions. This is manifested, first of all, in the unstable position of chamotte, it never managed to finally displace tarmac to the second position. There are monuments, the technical and technological schemes of which demonstrate a stable predominance of driftwood (Lemeshevichi). At other monuments (David-Gorodok, Gorodishche), along with recipes with predominance of chamotte, recipes with different ratios of dresva and chamotte coexist. There is a clear strengthening of the "fireclay" tradition from north to south.

Zarubinets pottery is also characterized by recipes with the presence of crushed bog iron ore. Ore always acted as an additional oatmealizing additive. It is a "capricious" opacifier and it was usually added in a very finely ground state in very small quantities

- no more than 3-5%. The only exception is Chaplin, where the share of ore in the composition of molding masses, especially unblocked vessels reaches 10-15%. This is due to the use of highly plastic clays with a low content of natural otoschitel. The basic recipe of Chaplin ceramics is clay + clay loam + ore. Recipes with the presence of ore are not recorded in every monument. The use of such a technically difficult heating agent as bog ore testifies to the high professional skill of local potters.

It should be noted some peculiarity in the composition of recipes of molding masses with crushed bog ore of the Upper Podniprovye and Pripyat Polesie. If the recipe: clay + tarmac + ore is present in the pottery of both regions, then with regard to the recipe: clay + tarmac + fireclay + ore there are some peculiarities in the ratio of special components. In particular, in the Upper Podneprovie there are complex recipes: clay + dresva + chamotte + ore and clay + dresva + ore + chamotte. The predominance of driftwood in these recipes is due to the fact that pottery of the Upper Podneprovie is characterized by the tradition of using driftwood as the main calcifying component. In Pripyat Polesie, fireclay is often used as the main peeling additive, while soda ash and ore occupy the second position.

In the Zarubinets time in the Pripyat pottery appears such a type of otoshchitel as dried clay or fragments of unburnt vessels - clay otoshchitel (Velemichi II, Lemeshevichi, Otverzhichi, Remel). The use of clay otoshchitel is not typical for pottery of the forest zone of Eastern Europe. There the role of an additional "soft" opacifier was performed by fireclay and ore. The tradition of using clay otoshchitel, as well as sand, has a southern origin and is connected with the southern forest-steppe and steppe tradition brought by the Zarubinsk people during their settlement up the Dnieper in the late 3rd-2nd centuries BC. In the compositions of molding masses clay otoshchitel replaced fireclay and occupied the second position after tarmac.

As for the recipes with the presence of organic otoshchitel, most likely, this type of otoshchitel is not typical for the ancient pottery in Belarus. Inclusions of plant and animal origin recorded in small quantities (not more than 1%) in the compositions of molding masses are not able to affect the quality of the mass and, therefore, they are not a thickening additive specially introduced for this purpose. Perhaps, their presence in the composition of ceramic masses of ancient vessels can be explained by their ritual purpose.

In the Zarubinets time, as before, pottery was fired in the fire, without special devices. Most often the firing of both chipped and unchipped ware took place in a reducing (smoky) gas environment. The seasoned oxidizing firing mode is more complicated, it has high requirements to the quality of fuel, long maintenance of stable temperature, etc. The firing mode was usually set and depended on many factors: the quality and thickness of vessels, the quality of fuel, the factor of cultural and technological traditions played a certain role. The firing temperature was determined by ancient potters "by eye". Apparently, the masters determined it by the color of firing products and the flame itself. Firing without special devices, the use of easy-melting clays, low temperatures and reducing gas environment - the technological chain of pottery of the forest belt in the Iron Age of Eastern Europe.

The study of the technology of ceramic complexes of the Zarubinets culture testifies to the preservation and further development of traditional techniques, and the emergence of new techniques associated with the introduction of their technological methods. The main direction of changes in ceramic production in this period is the improvement of the technology of processing raw materials and vessel surface, the search for optimal firing conditions. While preserving the diversity of technical methods in the processing of raw materials, generally recognized technological traditions with a wide spreading sphere are identified and actively function.

§ 3 Production of pottery among the tribes of the Hatch pottery culture (5th century B.C. - 5th century A.D.).

The culture of shaded pottery - one of the oldest and largest archaeological cultures of the Iron Age occupies a large territory of modern Lithuania, Latvia and Belarus. On the territory of Belarus the monuments of the culture of shaded pottery are concentrated in the central part of Belarus, including Upper Poneman, the eastern border runs along the middle and upper reaches of the Berezina River, in the south the monuments of the culture of shaded pottery reach the left bank of the Pripyat River.

Unfortunately, the technology of pottery production among the tribes of the hatching pottery culture has not been studied specifically. Only a small collection of ceramics from one of the southernmost settlement of the hatching pottery culture - Ivan settlement (left bank of the Pripyat River) - has been studied. In general, the issues of pottery production technology are presented on the basis of visual observations.

Potters of the tribes of the Hatch pottery culture in the territory of Belarus in the southern and central parts of the culture area used lake-alluvial clays, mainly of hydrous mica mineral composition. It is the hydrous mica component that determines the high plasticity and fusibility of the clay raw material, the qualities so necessary for ancient pottery. In the northern parts of the area leaner clay rocks of lake-glacial origin prevail.

Judging by visual observations and mineralogical and petrographic analysis of ceramic samples, the main special calcareous admixture in the composition of molding masses of ceramic vessels was crystalline rock gravel. Judging by the component composition (feldspars, quartz, mica), ordinary biotite granite, often with a high content of dark-colored mica - biotite, was used as a source rock for the production of the tresva. By coarseness, tarmac is subdivided into fine and medium (up to 1.9 mm), coarse (more than 2.0 mm). Some researchers believe that the dimensionality of the sands is a characteristic technological feature for a certain group of monuments, or even the region [Egoreychenko, 2006, p. 73]. Thus, the large size of cobbles prevails in the northern area of the culture of shaded ceramics (Eastern Lithuania, South-Eastern

Latvia) [Bobrinsky, 1978, p. 247; Vasks, 1991, pp. 67, 69], the further south, the smaller the cobbles in the molding mass [Egoreichenko, 2006, p. 73]. In fact, the dimensionality of the sands is not a cultural-territorial production feature in ancient pottery. First of all, in the north of Belarus, as well as in the territory of Eastern Lithuania and South-Eastern Latvia, strongly sandy lean clayey rocks of lake-glacial origin were used. Often natural non-plastic otoshchitel in such clays could reach 50-60 %, the size of mineral inclusions varied from fine to coarse and coarse-grained - up to 1.0-1.5 mm, with a considerable share of coarse-sized material. The finest grains of natural otoschist are practically unrolled, larger grains correspond to angularly rolled and semi-rolled forms. The distribution of natural clastic admixture is usually uniform. A noticeable degree of pelletization and uniform distribution are the main indicators allowing to distinguish the grains of natural otoshchitel from the grains of crystalline rocks released during crushing, which were specially introduced into the molding mass, however, it is often difficult to distinguish the natural otoshchitel from the specially introduced non-plastic admixture. In the southern regions of Belarus, plastic clays of lake-alluvial origin are widespread, mainly with hydrous-mica mineral composition with finer grain size of natural otoshchitel. Secondly, the dimensionality of tars also depended on the functional purpose of the vessel. For the manufacture of thin-walled vessels clay was specially tempered, cleaning from coarse inclusions, that is why the dough for such vessels is characterized by careful kneading and fine-sized otoschitelnye impurities. This is especially characteristic of tableware and ritual ware.

The second special oatmealizing additive found in the molding mass of vessels of the hatching pottery culture was fireclay. The use of fireclay is not typical for the northern regions of Belarus and the Baltic States. The use of fireclay in the southern regions is connected with the influence of southern local traditions, which were formed in the southern territories of modern Belarus in the Bronze Age. Additional "fireclay" impetus to the local pottery was introduced in the late 3rd - early 2nd centuries BC by the Zarubinets tribes. The settlement of the population of the shaded pottery culture among the local Pre-Lessian and Polesian tribes left its imprint on the traditional production patterns. In pottery this manifested itself in the use of chamotte as one of the components in complex recipes.

As a rule, chamotte was added in small quantities (about 3%) (Ivan) in a finely ground state (up to 1.0 mm at most). The addition of chamotte as part of the molding mass was recorded at the Palitskoe settlement [Loshenkov, 2000, p. 126]. A small addition of finely ground chamotte did not radically change the established "driftwood" tradition and at the same time was an illustration of the adaptation of foreign production traditions to local ones.

In the north of the region of distribution of monuments of the shaded pottery culture in the compositions of molding masses the presence of additives of organic origin (manure) was noted, mainly in Lithuania and southeastern Latvia [Bobrinsky, 1978, p. 247; Vasks, 1991, p. 67]. It is known that the introduction of organic otoshchitelnyh organic origin reduces the shrinkage of clay and gives the finished product more lightness. The use of such an otoshchit is especially relevant for heavy silted clay rocks of lake-glacial origin, which were widespread in this region. For areas where more plastic clays of lacustrine-alluvial origin were common, it is not technically feasible to use such a thickener. Obviously in this connection, this northern tradition, widespread in the Finno-Ugric environment, did not spread in the more southern lands of the territory of Belarus. The admixture of crushed plants, individual grains of cultivated cereals, often recorded in the compositions of molding masses of vessels of the Iron Age, including vessels of the hatching pottery culture, had no technical significance due to its insignificant share (about 1%) in the total composition of the ceramic mass.

At some monuments of the shaded pottery culture, inclusions of crushed iron ore as one of the special calcifying components (Palitskoe) were visually recorded in the molding masses [Loshenkov, 2000, p. 126]. Recipes including crushed iron ore appeared in Milograd pottery not earlier than IV-III centuries B.C. This is due to the fact that ore is a "capricious" otoschitel and requires special skills.

Subsequently, the Zarubinets potters mastered the skills of working with bog iron ore. The use of this type of special otoshchitel is apparently not typical for the pottery of the hatch pottery culture.

As everywhere in the pottery of the Eastern European forest zone era, the tribes of the Hatch pottery culture dominated the fire firing with low temperatures (up to 850°) and the prevalence of a reducing gas environment. The nature of the gas environment of ancient pottery is determined by the fresh fracture of the shard, because as a result of the long stay of the shard in moist layers of the earth there is a process of restoration of the original clay structure and the surface of the vessels, initially fired in the reduction firing, acquires a light color. If the degree of dehydration goes far, the ancient vessels become similar to weakly fired, although in fact the firing temperatures were sufficient to get a strong shard (above 500-550 ° C). In this regard, to make any classification of ancient tableware on the coloring of surfaces is inappropriate [Egoreychenko, 2006, p. 25, 75].

In general, the pottery of the tribes of the Hatch pottery culture fits within the framework of the region-wide tradition of pottery production characteristic of the forest zone of Eastern Europe. This tradition is characterized by the use of crystalline rock sands as the main component of the molding mass. Chalk was used both in regions with predominantly lean lake-glacial clay rocks (the northern part of the area of the shaded pottery culture) and in regions with more plastic lake-alluvial clay rocks. The share of the tars depends on the degree of sandiness of the initial clay rock and the presence of other special peeling components in the composition of the molding mass. Apparently, a simple recipe based on a clay binder and wooddressing was dominant in the pottery of the shaded pottery culture. Complex multi-component recipes were not common. In the Baltic region of the culture area and possibly at the extreme north-eastern sites of the culture in Belarus, ruminant dung was added to make the molding mass more plastic. In the extreme south of the culture area (the left bank of the Pripyat River), chamotte was additionally added to the molding masses in small quantities. The use of fireclay is connected with the settlement of the population of the shaded pottery culture among the local Polesian tribes. The influence of local pottery traditions could not but affect the traditional pottery production patterns of the Hatch pottery culture.

§ 4 Production of pottery in the tribes of the Abidnya culture (III-V cc.).

The advance of the post-Zarubinets population northward upstream of the Dnieper River in the early 1st millennium A.D. and direct contacts with the indigenous Baltic population led to the emergence of a new ethno-cultural massif in this region, whose tribes left Abidni type antiquities. The formed new cultural community did not lose the characteristic features of the Zarubinets antiquities, but they were somewhat simplified. This was especially evident in the ceramic complex. The assortment of tableware, especially tableware, was reduced. Jugs and mugs with handles practically disappeared, and the forms of bowls simplified. Roughly molded pots and baskets became predominant. The amount of lacquered ware was reduced to a minimum. On average, at each individual settlement, the amount of lacquered and under-lacquered ware does not exceed 5%, and there are monuments where single lacquered shards were found. The quality of glossing also deteriorated significantly.

The "coarsening" of pottery did not mean a regression in the production of ceramic vessels, a loss of the technological knowledge that the Zarubins brought with them. In the absence of a potter's wheel and the presence of only the simplest firing devices, they created high-quality, convenient tableware and fully satisfied the needs of the population. The interaction of local and foreign cultural traditions was not limited to external manifestations - new forms of ceramics, jewelry, etc., but reflected the general deep shifts in different spheres of material culture - metallurgy, pottery, etc., and contributed to the acceleration of their development. It is known that a certain historical level of production development is especially indicative of the stability in the choice of materials, as well as the stability of techniques

The skills were often retained and incorporated into local production. When tribes or population groups moved to other territories, these skills were often retained and incorporated into local production. In ceramic production, it concerned, first of all, the choice of raw materials, the selection of calcareous admixtures, recipes for the composition of molding masses.

Abidnensky potters used the same local clays, mainly of hydrosludic mineral composition, both for the production of unlacquered and lacquered ware. Usually these are lake-alluvial banded (due to seasonal accumulation of material) clayey rocks of Anthropogenic age, the admixture of non-plastic clastic clastic material in which, defined as a natural heater, did not exceed 30-40 %. According to their properties, they are raw materials suitable for the production of ceramic products.

Abidnya potters added granite grit, fireclay, and crushed bog ore (limonite) to the clay mass as artificial additives. Simple recipes consisting of a clay binder and one special additive are no longer found in the pottery of the Abidnya culture. All recipes of molding masses are multi-component, i.e. in addition to clay binder simultaneously contain several additives of inorganic origin. As in the previous times, the leading specializing peeling additive is still the sanddressing agent. Along with the common Zarubinets recipes of clay + sanddress + chamotte and clay + sanddress + ore, the recipe of clay + sanddress + ore + chamotte became widespread in this period. Obviously, the authors of this recipe were Milograd potters and its appearance, apparently, belongs to the period not earlier than IV-III centuries B.C., since it is at this time that recipes containing ore appear in Milograd pottery. In contrast to the more widespread recipe of clay + dresva + ore, the recipe of clay + dresva + ore + chamotte in the Milograd time is represented by single cases (Branches). It was not very popular among the potters of the Zarubinets culture tribes either. And only in the pottery of the Abidnya culture this recipe becomes the most widespread.

Despite the rather wide use of crushed iron ore as a special opacifier in pottery of the Iron Age tribes of the Byelorussian Podneprovye region, recipes with ore are not represented in every monument. Thus, for example, in the Zarubinets time at the settlement Chaplin and later, in the second quarter of the I millennium AD. - Abidnya settlement, recipes with crushed bog ore were absolutely predominant, whereas they were not found at all at neighboring monuments, such as the simultaneous Abidnya Simonovichi. Obviously, the reason for this is not only the presence of raw materials for otoshchitel near the settlements, but also some local technological peculiarities.

Moreover, fireclay and ore had the same technological functions and were interchangeable.

As a rule, fireclay and ore were finely ground to be used as a special opacifier. The use of finely ground otoshchitel is characteristic of Zarubinets pottery, especially in the production of chipped ware. Chamotte and ore were especially finely crushed, as it was impossible to crush crystalline rock tars into powder with the existing technical devices of those times. The use of finely crushed soft otoschitel, such as fireclay and ore, was of great technical importance. The fine particles of such an otoschitel are "blurred" in the surrounding clay substrate, which testifies to their active interaction with the surrounding mass during the firing process.

The Abydno potters, like their predecessors, fired pottery in open hearths. Such a firing device does not actually differ from an ordinary fire. It is not protected by any structures that would shelter it or somehow limit the firing area. These are open hearths at ground level and open hearths in hollows. This method of firing is predominant for the Iron Age of the forest belt. Firing in fire pits is evidenced both by the low firing temperatures and the unstable gas environment. It is not excluded that somewhat different types of devices could have been used for reduction firing, which functionally gravitated towards single-chamber closed furnaces, i.e. the firing zone was partially or completely covered by some stable (at least for the time of firing) external covering. Apparently, most of the single-chamber closed fixtures could be used not only for firing pottery but also for other purposes, although some may have served only for firing pottery.

The pottery of the Abidni culture tribes is an illustration of the synthesis of their predecessors' achievements. Despite the fact that in this period there is a sharp reduction in the production of lacquered ware, the skills developed in its manufacture are preserved. This period saw the final consolidation of the role of tarmac as the leading peeling admixture, the expansion of the range of peeling admixtures in one recipe, the wide and differentiated use of finely ground peeling agent (ore, fireclay), and the improvement of thermal treatment of pottery.

Dresva and recipes based on it dominated in pottery of the tribes of the neighboring Abidnya culture archaeological cultures of the second quarter of the 1st millennium A.D. of the forest belt - the late stages of shaded pottery and Dnieper-Dvinsky [Mitrofanov, 1978, p. 29, 100; Schmidt, 1992, p. 94-95] and then formed on their basis Banzerovo and Tushemlyan archaeological cultures of the third quarter of the 1st millennium A.D. [Krenke, Lopatin, 1997, p. 64; Lopatin, 1987, p. 85-91, 184-1181; Shadyra, 2006, p. 78]. [Krenke, Lopatin, 1997, p. 64; Lopatin, 1987, pp. 85-91, 184-188; Shadyra, 2006, p. 78]. The tradition of using tarmac as the main special ottoman component of molding masses is preserved in the Upper Podneprovie and in ceramic production among the tribes of the Kolochin culture [Lopatin, 1987, p. 85-91, 184-188; Makushshkau, 1985, p. 6; Makushnikov, 2016, p. 28].

§ 5 Production of pottery among the tribes of the third quarter of the 1st millennium A.D. in Belarus.

Unfortunately, the technological aspects of pottery production in the tribes of the third quarter of the 1st millennium A.D. in Belarus (the Praga, Kolochin, Bantser, and Tushemlyan archaeological cultures) have not been specifically considered. We can judge about the level of pottery in these tribes only by fragmentary visual observations. However, it is impossible to ignore the consideration of the peculiarities of the technological process of pottery production in these tribes. It is especially relevant for the south of the territory of Belarus, where as a result of the influence of the Slavic Praga (antiquities of Korczak type in the territory of the Pripyat Polesie) on the local pottery traditions, the production "conflict" between dresva and chamotte was significantly aggravated. It should be noted that this concerned not only Pripyat Polesie, where the struggle for priority between "fireclay" and "dresvyany" traditions has a long history, but also in the Middle Podneprovie, where fireclay traditions used to prevail. Judging by visual observations, it is the predominance of driftwood in the composition of molding masses that is revealed on many Prague monuments of the Pripyat Polesie (Petrikov, Snyadin-1, Snyadin-2) [Vyarhei, 1999, p. 325]. A similar picture was observed in the pottery of the neighboring Kolochyn culture [Makuśśśkau, 1999, p. 354]. In the area of the Penkovo culture - in the Middle Podneprovye and Podesenye local potters also used dresva in addition to chamotte when making ceramic masses [Prikhodniuk, 1998, p. 33].

The use of fireclay as a special opacifier in the composition of molding masses in the pottery of the Pripyat Polesie has ancient roots - from the Bronze Age (the first half of the II millennium BC). In the southern regions of Central Belarus chamotte appears as an influence of southern production traditions, the farther to the north, the weaker is this influence. Chamot was not used in pottery of the northern Belarusian lands. Only after the turn of the A.D., with the extinction of the classical Zarubinets culture, the production picture of pottery in Belarus began to change. Chamot never became the main special additive in pottery of any of the Iron Age cultures in Belarus. After the turn of the AD, chamot in ancient Belarusian pottery rapidly loses its position. If in the Zarubinets period chamot prevailed on a number of monuments of the Pripyat Polesie, especially in the extreme south of the right bank of the Pripyat (David-Gorod), it is not typical for the pottery of the Praga culture.

In central and northern Belarus in the third quarter of the 1st millennium A.D., the ancient established "wood" tradition in pottery continued to exist. The pottery of the Kolochi culture, which was formed on the basis of Abidni antiquities, absorbed the production traditions of its predecessors. Apparently, the leading recipe for molding masses in the Kolochi pottery continued to be, as well as in the predecessors, the recipe of clay + sod + fireclay. Chamotte was the main special additive. It is not excluded the use of crushed bog ore as a non-main special additive.

The pottery of the Banzer culture was a continuation of the traditions of the shaded pottery culture and Dnieper Dvina pottery, which was indiscriminately dominated by the "driftwood" tradition. The use of chamotte as a non-essential special additive in complex multi-component recipes in Banzer pottery remains questionable. It is known that in the pottery of the shaded pottery culture, chamotte in complex recipes is found in the south of the area under the influence of the Zarubinets and post-Zarubinets traditions.

It is not excluded that this tradition was transferred to Banzer pottery especially in the south of the area. The use of sand as a special peeling additive [Shadyra, 2006, p. 72] was probably not widespread.

The conditions of pottery firing in the third quarter of the 1st millennium A.D. in Belarus remained the same. Ware continued to be fired in the conditions of the fire. This is evidenced by a moderate degree of alteration of the clay raw material, occurring at low firing temperatures of 500-700 (750°C). The prevailing gas environment of firing, as in the early period, was a reducing gas environment.

Thus, the pottery of the cultures of the third quarter of the 1st millennium A.D. in the territory of Belarus (Praga, Kolochi, Banzer) generally preserved the traditions formed by their predecessors. The region-wide scheme based on clay binder, tarmac and chamotte, which emerged and finally consolidated in Milograd pottery by the 3rd century B.C., was characterized by exceptional production stability and wide application. Taresva strengthens its position as the main special additive in the composition of the molding mass. The use of crushed granite rock as an artificial opacifier proved to be a suitable additive for local, predominantly clayey rocks, which allowed this tradition to become firmly and permanently established in the pottery of all archaeological cultures from the Neolithic period onwards. The use of quartz sand as a special calcifying additive for pottery was not characteristic of any of the archaeological cultures. Visually defined sand admixture as an artificial opacifier of the molding mass, most often, represents isolated grains of granite crumbs (dresva) or sandy-silty admixture, initially present in the clay raw material (natural opacifier of the clay mass).

§ 6 Production of ceramic tableware among the tribes of the last quarter of the 1st millennium A.D. in Belarus.

The issues of ceramic ware manufacturing technology of the tribes of the last quarter are considered on the materials of the Luka-Rajkovetska culture at the ancient settlement and the Gorodishche settlement (right bank of the Pripyat River).

Judging by the materials of the settlement, potters in the last quarter of the first millennium A.D. used more diverse sources of raw materials, including clay rocks with a high content of kaolinite-montmorillonite component. Most often these clays were used for preparation of such a special additive as clay otoschitel. According to the degree of plasticity it is also possible to distinguish clays of two varieties, one of them is highly plastic with the content of natural fine clastic non-plastic admixture not more than 7-10%, the second - thinner medium plastic clays with the content of natural otoshchitel 15-35%. Most often clays of the second type were used.

The main special peeling additives in Slavic ceramics of the last quarter of the 1st millennium AD, as well as in the previous periods, are sanddust and fireclay. The main recipe for the composition of molding masses continues to be the recipe of clay + claydust + fireclay.

At the same time, in contrast to previous periods, other special peeling additives are more widely used, in particular, clay peeler. The use of clay otoshchitel is a characteristic feature of Polesian pottery. This type of ottoman is not typical for the Podneprovie region. Clay otoshchitel appeared in the Pripyat pottery as early as in the Zarubinets time. Apparently, its use is a tradition brought by the Zarubinets to the local pottery from the southern regions. Initially, this production tradition was not widely used. However, the position of clay otoshchitel in the Polesie pottery gradually strengthened. Already in the last centuries of the 1st millennium A.D. it firmly occupied its niche in the general technical and technological scheme of local pottery. It is connected with high technological characteristics of the clay pottery itself and availability of raw materials for its production. As a raw material we used clays in which along with hydromica kaolinite-montmorillonite component was present in considerable quantity. Kaolin clays are more refractory than hydromica clays, their structure changes insignificantly during fire firing. The clay otoschitel performed the same technological functions as fireclay and was a "soft" otoschitel. The fusion of the traditions of using fireclay and clay otoshchit led to the appearance of low-temperature fireclay, which is a piece of clay rock or molding mass, fired at low temperatures, which is part of the improvement of the technological scheme of ceramic ware production. It is not excluded that ancient potters considered high-temperature and low-temperature fireclay and clay opacifier as varieties of one opacifier.

Crushed iron bog ore and quartz sand were occasionally continued to be used as secondary special peeling agents. Finely crushed bog ore as an additional oatmealizer was used in Upper Dnieper and Polesie pottery and is known from the early Milograd period. Crushed bog ore was used as an additional "soft" opacifier instead of chamotte, although there are known recipes where chamotte and ore were used simultaneously.

Quartz sand was used in Polesian pottery since the early Milograd time (Lemeshevichi), possibly even earlier. It was a calibrated material of gravel and sand mainly of coarse and coarse dimensions (up to 2.0-2.5 mm). For the Upper Dnieper pottery in the Early Iron Age this type of otoshchitel is not characteristic. Apparently, it was not widespread in the Polesian pottery either. The overestimated role of sandy otoshchitel as a special additive is explained by the difficulty of separating the special sand additive and natural sandy-silty admixture, especially during visual examination.

The technical and technological schemes of pottery production in Belarus became much more complicated in the last quarter of the 1st millennium A.D. compared to the previous periods. The formulation of molding masses was considerably expanded, especially in the southern regions. First of all, due to the expansion of recipes with the presence of clay otoshchitel. Nevertheless, the general technological tradition was preserved, it was reflected in the preservation of the leading positions of the recipe: clay + tarmac + fireclay. The leading positions of this recipe were preserved in pottery in Belarus throughout the Iron Age, only some differences are observed in the ratio of clay and chamotte. If in the Milograd time, both in the Podneprovye and Polesie the leading special component in the recipe was granite tarmac, then in the Zarubinets time the accents shifted somewhat. This was due to the fact that the Zarubinets tribes, settling upstream along the Dnieper and its large tributaries (Pripyat, Berezina), brought with them the tradition of extensive use of chamotte. Nevertheless, the technical and technological scheme based on the predominance of driftwood proved to be stable. In the Upper Podneprovie it completely preserved its positions, in the Pripyat Polesie, which is territorially located closer to the fireclay forest-steppe, there is a coexistence of mixed recipes with different ratios of tarmac and fireclay. A similar situation in the Pripyat basin was observed in the last quarter of the first millennium AD.

As for the clay otoshchitel, its position in the Polesian pottery at the end of the 1st millennium A.D. was considerably strengthened. If in the Zarubinets time only one recipe with the presence of clay opacifier is reliably recorded - clay + clay dresva + clay opacifier, in the last centuries of the 1st millennium A.D. on the example of Gorodishche pottery we know four recipes for the composition of molding masses with clay opacifier. There is one simple recipe: clay + clay opener and three complex recipes: clay + fireclay + clay opener; clay + wood chips + fireclay + clay opener; clay + clay opener + fireclay + wood chips + ore. All of them are based on local recipes.

The peculiarity of the Gorodishche pottery in this period is the change of the position of clay otoshchitel in the composition of a complex recipe. If earlier, in the Zarubinets time, clay thickener in all multi-component recipes was present as a minor additive, now in some cases it is the main thickening component.

In the pottery of the more northern regions of Belarus in the last quarter of the 1st millennium A.D. the same situation continued. Dresva was still the dominant special leaning additive. Even the radical revolution in the pottery of the forest belt of Eastern Europe in the IX-X (XI) centuries, associated with the industrial development of the potter's wheel, did not produce significant changes in the formulation of molding masses. For example, the early round pottery of the Chaplin settlement (Podneprovye) has the same recipe as in the Milograd and Zarubinets times - clay + loam + ore. Finely crushed granite loam was used for the ceramics of the X-XIII cc. of ancient Novogrudok as the main leaning admixture of the molding mass for all categories of ware [Malevskaya-Malevich, 2005, p. 17]. Dresva is typical for the ceramics of other towns and rural settlements of the 10th-13th centuries in Belarus.

Only in the XVI century, when the foot potter's wheel finally replaced the hand wheel, there were changes related to bringing the technical parameters of the wheel in line with the technological properties of the molding mass. In ceramic masses, only fine shakers were used, sand gradually displaced tarmac, and clay concentrates formed from several types of clay without the addition of non-plastic impurities became widespread.

This process can be traced on the example of medieval ceramics of northeastern Belarus, where the main shrinking impurities were sand and finely ground fireclay [Levko, 1992, p. 11]. However, the process of replacing tarmac was long. As early as in the XVI-XVII centuries, according to the data of mineralogical and petrographic analysis of ceramic ware from Mogilev and Mstislavl, this type of heating agent was used in the manufacture of both non-irrigated and irrigated wares [Zdanovich, Trusau, 1993, p. 75]. Judging by ethnographic materials, tarmac is still used in artisanal pottery in Belarus [Miliuchenkov, 1984, p. 35].

In the last quarter of the 1st millennium A.D. the firing conditions remained the same. The pottery was still fired under fire conditions. This is evidenced by a moderate degree of change in the initial, mainly hydrous mica clay substance as a result of firing at low temperatures - 500-700 (750)°. The prevailing gas medium, as in the early period, was the reducing gas medium of firing. Often the firing medium is characterized as unstable (two-three-colored shards), which is often the case with fire firing. At the end of the 1st millennium A.D., kiln firing replaces fire firing. Temperatures of kiln firing do not differ from those of fire firing (up to 850°C). However, when firing in a kiln it is possible to maintain a stable gas environment, which leads to a more uniform calcination of the shard throughout its thickness and, consequently, to obtain better quality products at the output. However, low firing temperatures did not allow firing products made of refractory kaolinite clays. This became possible only with the spread of mountain firing. In particular, white linens made of kaolinite clays, which were characterized by high consumer characteristics, were widespread in the XVI-XVII centuries in many towns of Pripyat Polesie (Pinsk, Turov, David-Horodok), near which there are outcrops of such clays.

Conclusion.

Ceramic production in the economic life of tribes in the Iron Age occupies one of the most important places. It is in the peculiarities of the development of ceramic production that the nature of the process of deepening the specialization of production activity in the manufacture of products and the formation of the most progressive form of labor organization for this period - the craft - can be traced. Throughout the Iron Age and the Early Middle Ages (the middle of the first millennium B.C. - the first millennium A.D.), complex changes took place in the production activity of the population in the territory of Belarus, connected not just with progressive development, but with the gradual internal restructuring of its entire organization. As a result of deepening differentiation and specialization of ceramic production, the forms of labor organization, which can be characterized as pre-crafts, are singled out. An important moment in the emergence of craft forms of labor was the creation and consolidation of a region-wide technological scheme. However, only with the introduction of the technical base necessary for the existence of craft as a form of social organization of production (potter's wheel, kilns, potsherds), ceramic production becomes a craft. On the territory of Belarus we can speak about pottery as a craft form of production from the end of the IX-X centuries.

Throughout the entire existence of ceramic ware production, starting from the Neolithic Age, there was cultural and production continuity in the territory of Belarus. During the whole period under consideration, there was an inflow and outflow of the population of different ethnic origin in the territory of Belarus. Each new influx of population came to these lands with its own production traditions, including the production of pottery. These production traditions brought a new impetus to the development of local ceramic production. However, on the other hand, they were confronted with the established traditions of the former population, adapted to local conditions and local sources of raw materials.

The merger of local and introduced traditions led to the fact that often the introduced traditions lost their relevance and gave way to local traditions, tied to local conditions and sources of raw materials, in other cases it led to the emergence of some new trends in the technology of pottery production. An example of the first variant is the loss of the position of chamotte as the main shrinking component in the Zarubinets pottery of the Middle Sub-Dnieper, associated with the settlement of the Zarubinets up the Dnieper and its main tributaries. The arrival of the Zarubinets in the Upper Sub-Dnieper region, where for a long time the recipe of pottery production was dominated by chamotte, perfectly adapted to the local easy-melting, mainly hydrous clayey rocks, did not allow chamotte to displace chamotte to the second position. On the other hand, local potters knew and appreciated the excellent technological properties of chamotte, which eventually led to the consolidation of the all-regional recipe: clay + tarmac + chamotte. On the right bank of the Pripyat River, the territory directly adjacent to the "chamotte" forest-steppe, the position of chamotte in local pottery, starting from the Bronze Age, was the strongest. This was reflected in the ratio of chamotte and fireclay in the region-wide recipe, when chamotte often occupied the first positions in the region-wide recipe: clay + fireclay + chamotte + chamotte. An example of the second variant was the emergence and spreading in the Polesie Zarubinets pottery of such a type of opacifier as clay opacifier and later the emergence of a new type of special opacifying admixture as low-temperature fireclay. The merger of the traditions of using chamotte and clay pouring agent and the emergence of low-temperature chamotte are part of the improvement of the technological scheme of ceramic ware production. The technological qualities of the clay opacifier and low-temperature fireclay were so similar that local potters regarded them as varieties of the same type of special opacifier.

Literature:

1. Bobrinsky A.A. Pottery of Eastern Europe. Sources and Methods of Study / ed. by S.A. Pletneva. - Moscow: Nauka, 1978. - 272 c.

2. Vasks A.V. Ceramics of the Late Bronze Age and Early Iron Age / ed. by J.J. Graudonis. - Riga: Zinatne, 1991. - 198 c.

3. Vyarhei V.S. ПОМНікі youpu Pray-Korchak i Luyu-Raikavetskaya // Archealoi Belarus u 4 t. / nauk. ed. B.1. Shadyra, V.S. Vyarhei. - Mshsk: Belarus. nauvuka, 1999. - T. 2: Zhalezny vek i early särädnya vechcha. - C. 317-348.

4. Egoreychenko A. A. The most ancient settlements of the Belarusian Polesie (VII-VI centuries BC - II century AD) / scientific ed. V.V. Sedov. Sedov. - Minsk, 1996. - 148 p.: ill.

5. Egoreychenko A. A. Cultures of shaded ceramics. - Minsk: BSU, 2006. - 207 p.: ill.

6. Zdanovich N.1., Trusau A.A. Belaruskaya potvanaya keramja XI- XVIII st.st. / edited by G.V. Shtykhav. G.V. Shtykhav. - Mshsk: Navuka i tehshka, 1993. - 183 p.: w.

7. Isayenko V.F. Neolithic ceramics // Belarusian old age. Materials of the archealogy of the BSSR and other countries: Collection of articles / edited by L.D. Pobal i sh. Pobal i sh. - Mshsk, 1972. - C. 45-68.

8. Kalechits E.G. Ceramics of the Upper Dnieper culture // Gyvenvieciu ir keramikos raida balta zemese: Collected articles / edited by A.Girininkas. - Vilnius: Savastis, 194. - C. 133-147.

9. Kasparova K.V. Zarubinetsky burial ground Velemichi // Archaeological Collection of the State Hermitage. - Л., 1972. - Vyp. 14. - C. 53-111.

10. Kasparova K.V. New materials of the Otverzhichi burial ground and some questions of relative chronology of the Zarubinets culture of Polesie // Archaeological Collection of the State Hermitage. - Л., 1976. - Vyl. 17. - C. 35-66.

11. Kasparova K.V. Zarubinets settlement Remel // Archaeological Collection of the State Hermitage. - Л., 1987. - Vyp. 28. - C. 52-70.

12. Krenke N.A., Lopatin N.V. Petrographic study of ceramics from the settlement of Dyakov and Tushemlya // Russian Archaeology. - M., 1997. - № 1. - C. 60-67.

13. Krywalcavich M.M. Aziannoye-1 - a settlement of the Bronze Age on the Palesia byunachy // Mataryaly p archealogy Belarus / edited by A.G. Kalechyts. A.G. Kalechyts. - Mlnsk, 1999. - Vyp. 2. - 108 c. ш.

14. Lashankou M.1. Maternal culture and occupation of the population / Section 2. 2. The Mshagrad and Pamor cultures // Archaeology of Belarus U 4 vol. - T. 2: The Iron Age and the Early Middle Ages / edited by V.1. B.1. Shadyry, V.S. Vyarhei. - Mshsk: Belaruskaya nauvuka, 1999. - C. 46-70.

15. Lopatin N. V. To the correlation of ceramics of the upper layers of Tushemli, Demidovka and Kolochin (experience of attracting some data on technology) // Socio-economic development of ancient societies and archaeology: Collected articles / ed. by V.S. Olkhovsky. - Moscow: Institute of Archaeology, 1987. - C. 85-91, 184-188.

16. Levko O.N. Medieval pottery of north-eastern Belarus / scientific editor G.V. Shtykhov. - Minsk: Navuka i tehshka, 1992. - 127 c.

17. Loshenkov M.1. Gorodishchi of the Milograd culture of the eastern part of the Belarusian Polesie: Author's thesis ..., Cand. of Historical Sciences: 07.00.06. - Kiev, 1990. - 22 c.

18. Loshenkov M.I. Palitskoe settlement // Is baltu kulturos istorijos. - Vilnius, 2000. - C. 125-140.

19. Loshenkov M.I. Mounds of the Milograd culture on the territory of Belarus. - Minsk: Minsk factory of color printing, 2011. - 406 c.

20. Makushshkau A.A. Kalochyn culture // Archealopia Belarus U 4 vol. - T. 2: The Iron Age and Early Middle Ages / edited by V.1. B.1. Shadyry, V.S. Vyarhei. - Mshsk: Belaruskaya nauvuka, 1999. - C. 348-359.

21. Makushnikov O. Gomel Podneprovye in V - middle of XIII century. Socio-economic, ethnic, cultural history. - LAP LAMBERT Academic Publishing, 2016. - 566 c.

22. Malevskaya-Malevich M.V. Ceramics of the West Russian cities of the X- XIII cc. / Ed. by M.V. Malyevich. C. V. Beletsky. - Proceedings. - VOL. XVII. - St. Petersburg: Nestor-Istory Publishing House, 2005. - 159 c.

23. Melnikovskaya O.N. The tribes of southern Belorussia in the Early Iron Age / ed. by Yu.V. Kukharenko. - Moscow: Nauka, 1967. - 194 p.: ill.

24. Milyuchenkov S.N. Belarusian folk pottery. - Minsk: Science and Technology, 1984. - 183 p.: ill.

25. Mitrofanov A.G. Iron Age of Middle Belorussia (VII-VI centuries BC - VIII century AD) / scientific ed. by G.V. Shtykhov. - Minsk: Science and Technology, 1978. - 160 p.: ill.

26. Pachkova S. P. Gospodarstvo schehchnoslov'yanskikh tribes at the turn of our1 era (after the materials of Zarubinets culture) / ed. by V.Y. Dovzhenok. Dovzhenok. - Kshv: Naukova Dumka, 1974. - 135 c.

27. Prikhodniuk O. M. Penkovo culture (cultural and archaeological aspect of the study) / ed. by A.Z. Vinnikov. - Voronezh: Voronezh University, 1998. - 170 c.

28. Pobol L. D. New Zarubinets burial grounds in the Turovshchina / New data on the Zarubinets culture in the Podneprovye // Materials and studies on the archeology of the USSR / ed. by P.N. Tretyakov. - L.: Nauka, 1969. - № 160. - C. 119-130.

29. Pobol L.D. Archaeological monuments of Belarus: Iron Age / scientific ed. M.A. Tkachev. - Minsk: Science and Technology, 1983. - 456 p.: ill.

30. Rassadin S. E. Milograd culture (actual problems of research): Autoref. dis.... Candidate of Historical Sciences: 07.00.06. - Kiev, 1989. - 20 c.

31. Charniausz M.M. Nealgg Belarusian Panyamonnya / ed. by D.Y. Tsyalepn. D.Y. Tsyalepn. - Minsk: Navuka i tehshka, 1979. - 144 p.: w.

32. Shadyra V.1. Belaruskae Padzvshne (I thousand years). - Mshsk, 2006. - 150 p.: il.

33. Schmidt E.A. Tribes of the upper Dnieper before the formation of the Old Russian state. I. Dnieper-Dvinsky tribes (VIII c. BC - III c. AD) - M.: Prometheus, 1992. - 208 p.; ill.

Printed by Books on Demand GmbH, Norderstedt / Germany